SCHUBERT

Nine Short Piano Pieces

Edited and annotated by

HOWARD FERGUSON

THE ASSOCIATED BOARD OF
THE ROYAL SCHOOLS OF MUSIC

© 1981 by The Associated Board of the Royal Schools of Music

Uniform with this edition

SCHUBERT

edited by Howard Ferguson

Complete Pianoforte Sonatas
(including the unfinished works)
Volumes I, II & III

Three Piano Pieces, D.946

Fantasy in C ('The Wanderer'), D.760

Moments Musicaux, D.780

Impromptus, D.899

Impromptus, D.935

Variations, D.156 & 576

Thirty-three Dances

CONTENTS

INTRODUCTION

This volume contains nine short pieces by Schubert for which there was no suitable place in the other volumes of the Associated Board's edition of Schubert's Pianoforte Works. They span most of his creative life, from the *Andante in C, D.29*, written at the age of 15, to the *Allegretto in C minor, D.915*, composed only eighteen months before his death; thus they provide a miniature survey of the solo works he wrote for his own beloved instrument. Particulars are as follows:

1. ANDANTE IN C, D.29
Sources. A, Autograph: Vienna, Stadtbibliothek, MH 146/c. B, 1st edition: *Gesammtausgabe* Series XI/9; Breitkopf & Härtel, Leipzig 1888. The present edition follows A. [Suggested tempo: ♪=c.88]

Schubert's own piano version of a rejected slow movement for his unfinished String Quartet in C, D.32.

2. ADAGIO IN G, D.178
Sources. A, Autograph: Vienna, Stadtbibliothek, MH 150/c. B, 1st edition: *Gesammtausgabe* Series XXI/22; Breitkopf & Härtel, Leipzig 1897. The present edition follows A. [Tempo: ♩=c.72]

Both A & B also contain an unfinished version of the piece, which starts with a similar theme but continues differently. It breaks off at the end of its b.60, just as a recapitulation of the opening has begun.

3 & 4. TWO SCHERZOS, D.593
Sources. A, Autograph: lost. B, 1st edition: *Zwei Scherzi . . . Nachgelassenes Werk*; J. P. Gotthard, Vienna 1871, plate No. 161. The present edition follows B. [Tempo: No. 1 ♩=c.144, No. 2 ♩=c.160, Trio ♩=c.144]

In the 1st edition, and almost all subsequent ones, the repeats are printed in full, even in the Da Capos. Doubtless this was a publisher's dodge for increasing the size of what would otherwise have been a meagre volume. Schubert would never have bothered to write them thus, or intended the repeats to have been made in the Da Capos.

The Trio of Scherzo II reappears in a variant form as the Trio of the Menuett in the Sonata in E flat, D.568.

5. MARCH IN E, D.606
Sources. A, Autograph: lost. B, 1st edition: *Marsch sammt Trio . . . von Franz Schubert aus dessen Nachlasse*; Artaria & Co., Vienna [1840], plate No. 3142. The present edition follows B. [Tempo: ♩=c.144]

Though Schubert wrote at least seventeen Marches for piano duet, this is the only surviving one for piano solo.

6. VARIATION IN C MINOR ON A WALTZ BY DIABELLI, D.718
Sources. A, Autograph: Vienna, Oesterreichische Nationalbibliothek, MHs.18371. B, 1st edition: *Vaterländischer Künstlerverein Veränderungen . . . über ein vorgelegtes Thema . . . 2te Abteilung;* A. Diabelli & Co., Vienna [1824], plate No. 1381. The present edition follows A. [Tempo: ♩=c.144]

In 1819 the publishers Cappi & Diabelli invited a number of composers to write a single variation each on a perky 32-bar Waltz by Diabelli. Beethoven characteristically produced a gigantic masterpiece, the *33 Variations on a Waltz by Anton Diabelli*, Op.120, which was published as a separate volume in 1823. The more modest contributions of fifty other composers,

two of whom were Schubert and the 11-year-old Liszt, were issued a year later in the companion volume mentioned above.

7. HUNGARIAN MELODY IN B MINOR, D.817
Sources. A, Autograph: Private collection, Geneva; facsimile in *Studia Musicologica,* III; Budapest 1962, pp. 91-93. B, 1st edition: *Ungarische Melodie für Klavier von Franz Schubert,* ed. O. E. Deutsch; Edition Strache No.20, Vienna 1928. The present edition follows the facsimile of A. [Tempo: ♩=c.92; from b.78, ♩=c.72]

This is a shorter, earlier version of the 3rd movement of the *Divertissement à l'hongroise,* D.818, for piano duet. It was written at Zseliz, a country seat of Count Johann Karl Esterházy, where Schubert was engaged during the summer months as piano teacher to the Count's daughters Marie and Karoline.

8. ALBUMLEAF IN G, D.844
Sources. A, Autograph: lost; photocopy, Berlin, Staatsbibliothek Preussischer Kulturbesitz, N.Mus.Nachl. 10,126. B, 1st edition: *Gesammtausgabe* Series XXI/31; Breitkopf & Härtel, Leipzig 1897. The present edition follows the photocopy of A. [Tempo: ♩=c.126]

Written in the autograph album of Anna Mayerhofer von Grünbühel, née Hönig (1803-88). A drawing of her by Schubert's friend Mortiz von Schwind is reproduced in O. E. Deutsch's *Schubert: a documentary biography;* Dent, London 1946, facing p.656.

9. ALLEGRETTO IN C MINOR, D.915
Sources. A, Autograph: Private collection, Thun. B, 1st edition: *Allegretto für Pianoforte . . . (Nachgelassenes Werk);* J. P. Gotthard, Vienna 1870, plate No. 99 The present edition follows B. [Tempo: ♩.=c.66]

Written in the autograph album of Ferdinand Walcher (1799-1873), a lawyer and amateur singer. In B the repeat of each section except the 2nd is printed in full. But the engraver forgot to include the double-bar and repeat-marks of present b.8, which were needed to correspond with those of b.30.

THIS EDITION
In the present edition numbered footnotes are concerned with textual matters, and lettered footnotes with the interpretation of ornaments, etc. Redundant accidentals have been omitted. Editorial accidentals, notes, rests, dynamics, etc., are printed either in small type or within square brackets, and editorial slurs, ties, and 'hairpin' *cresc.* and *dim.* signs are crossed with a small vertical line. Curved brackets indicate that a note should not be struck. Occasionally the original disposition of notes on the two staves has been altered when this might make them easier to read. The fingering throughout is editorial. Metronome marks within square brackets in the section above are offered as editorial suggestions: they are neither authoritative nor binding.

Thanks are due to the following for providing photocopies of autographs or allowing access to 1st editions, and for giving permission for their use in preparing the present volume: the Stadtbibliothek, Vienna; the Oesterreichische Nationalbibliothek, Vienna; the Staatsbibliothek Preussischer Kulturbesitz, Berlin; the British Library Board; and the Provost and Fellows of King's College, Cambridge.

HOWARD FERGUSON
Cambridge 1981

1. ANDANTE in C

D. 29

9 September 1812

Andante

2. ADAGIO in G
D.178

8 April 1815

(c) ♪ (d) gracenotes before the beat.

1) B. 55, r.h. beat 3: demi-semiquaver sextuplet in the autograph, but with the lowest beam stroked out.

3. SCHERZO in B flat
D. 593/1

November 1817

4. SCHERZO in D flat

D. 593/2

November 1817

(b) gracenotes before the beat.

Fine

TRIO

Scherzo D.C. al Fine senza replica

5. MARCH in E

D. 606

Allegro con brio

1818 ?

1) B.15, l.h. chord 2, lower line: E misprinted as D (sharp).
2) B.17, r.h. chord 3: E sharp misprinted as E double-sharp.
3) B.19, r.h. note 2: E sharp misprinted as E double-sharp.
4) B.27, l.h. chords 1 & 2, lowest line: C (sharp) misprinted as D (sharp).

A.B.1768

TRIO
legato sempre

Basso stacc.

sempre stacc.

[Fine]

Marcia Da Capo

5) Bb. 77-84, the r.h. phrasing (probably mistakenly — see bb. 53-60) is:-

6) B. 80, l.h. chord 2, lower line: E (flat) misprinted as D (flat).

A. B. 1768

6. VARIATION in C minor
on a Waltz by Diabelli
D. 719

March 1821

(a) for small hands: (b) for small hands: l.h.

7. HUNGARIAN MELODY

D. 817

2 September 1824

(a) short gracenote.

1) Bb. 13-15 & 61-63: *un poco rit.* and *a tempo* are taken from the duet version, D.818.

2) B.71: though not marked in either version, a [*rall.*] seems to be needed in bb.71-2, leading to [Meno mosso, ♩=c.72] at b.73.

8. ALBUMLEAF in G

D. 844

16 April 1825

9. ALLEGRETTO in C minor
D. 915

26 April 1827

1) B.32, r.h. chord 1: in the source there are no naturals to the Bs; but the D natural in the l.h. makes B flats most improbable.

Printed in England by Caligraving Limited Thetford Norfolk   A.B.1768

1:03